S0-BOE-558

MAGIC CASTLE READERS®

Yes, No, Little Hippo

A book about safety

BY JANE BELK MONCURE • ILLUSTRATED BY SUSAN DeSANTIS

The Child's World

Published by The Child's World®
1980 Lookout Drive • Mankato, MN 56003-1705
800-599-READ • www.childsworld.com

Acknowledgments
The Child's World®: Mary Berendes, Publishing Director
The Design Lab: Design
Jody Jensen Shaffer: Editing
Derrick Chow: Color

ISBN 9781623235710
LCCN 2013931412

Printed in the United States of America
Mankato, MN
July 2013
PA02177

Did you know...

A library is a magic castle with many Word Windows in it?

What is a Word Window?

If you said, "A book," you're right!

A book is a Word Window because the words and pictures let you look and see many things. Books are your windows to the wide, wide world around you.

The Library
Is a Magic Castle

Come to the Magic Castle
When you are growing tall.
Rows and rows of Word Windows
Line every single wall.
They reach up high,
As high as the sky,
And you'll want to open them all.
For every time you open one,
A new adventure has begun.

3

Beth opened a Word Window.
Here is what she read:

One night, Little Hippo said,
"I will jump on my bed." He jumped very high.

"No, no, Little Hippo," said his sister.
"It is not safe to play that way."

But Little Hippo went on jumping.
He jumped higher and higher.

Little Hippo jumped too high.
He fell off the bed and onto the floor.

Mama Hippo picked him up.
"No, no, Little Hippo," she said.
"Beds are not for jumping. Beds are for sleeping."

She kissed the bump on his head.
Then she tucked Little Hippo safely in bed.

The next day Little Hippo said,
"I will climb on a chair. I will climb very high."

"No, no, Little Hippo," said his brother.
"It is not safe to play that way."

But Little Hippo went on climbing.
He climbed higher and higher.

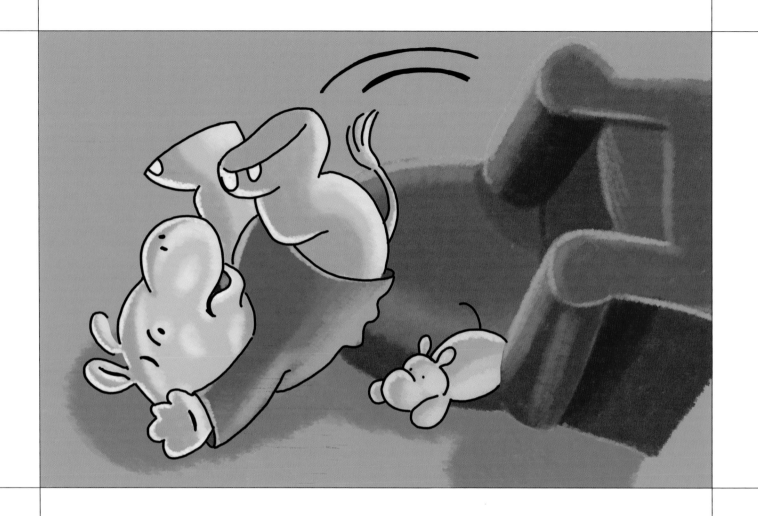

Little Hippo climbed too high.
The chair tipped over.
Little Hippo fell onto the floor.

Mama Hippo picked him up.
"No, no, Little Hippo," she said.
"Chairs are not for climbing. Chairs are for sitting."

She kissed the bump and sent Little Hippo
outside to play.

Little Hippo saw a friend.
"Let's ride our bikes," said the friend.

"I can ride very fast!" said Little Hippo.
He hopped on his bike and went very fast
down the hill.

"No, no, Little Hippo," said his friend.
"It is not safe to play that way."

But Little Hippo went faster and faster
down the hill. He went so fast, he took a spill.

Papa Hippo picked him up.
"No, no, Little Hippo," said Papa.
"Riding too fast is not a safe way to play."

"I always hear, 'No, no,'" said Little Hippo.
"What can I play so that you will say,
  'Yes, Yes! That's the way?'"

"Come with me," said Papa.
And off they went to the park.

Did Little Hippo jump at the park? Yes. Yes.
He jumped rope instead of jumping
on his bed.

Did he climb at the park? Yes. Yes.
He climbed high on the jungle gym
instead of a chair.

Did he ride his bike safely down a hill
without a spill? Yes, he did.

Then Papa said, "Let's go for a boat ride in the park."

Did Little Hippo put on a life jacket?
Yes, he did.

"We can do one more thing," Papa said.
"Let's ride in the cars," said Little Hippo.

Did he fasten his seat belt?
Yes, he did.

Did Little Hippo have fun at the park?
Can you guess?
Yes! Yes!

Questions and Activities

(Write your answers on a sheet of paper.)

1. In one sentence, tell what this book is about.
   Name three ways the author tells the book's main idea.

2. Describe Little Hippo. Write two things about him.

3. Where does this story start out? Where does the story end?
   How are these two places different?

4. Did this story have any words you don't know?
   How can you find out what they mean?

5. Name two things you learned about being safe.
   What else would you like to know?